21st Century Skills **INNOVATION** *Library*

Golf

by K. C. Kelley

CHERRY
LAKE
Publishing

Published in the United States of America by Cherry Lake Publishing
Ann Arbor, Michigan
www.cherrylakepublishing.com

Content Adviser: Thomas Sawyer, EdD, Professor of Recreation and Sport Management, Indiana
State University

Design: The Design Lab

Cover and page 3, ©Andrew Barker, used under license from Shutterstock, Inc.; page 4, ©Corbis
Premium RF/Alamy; page 6, ©iStockphoto.com/jvoisey; page 9, ©OJO Images Ltd/Alamy; page 10,
©RTimages, used under license from Shutterstock, Inc.; page 13, ©iStockphoto.com/davejkahn; page
14, ©FloridaStock, used under license from Shutterstock, Inc.; page 17, ©VINCENT GIORDANO, used
under license from Shutterstock, Inc.; page 19, ©Paul Laragy, used under license from Shutterstock,
Inc.; page 21, ©Content Mine International/Alamy; page 22, ©iStockphoto.com/russellillig; page 24,
©iStockphoto.com/sonyae; page 25, ©Stuart Abraham/Alamy; page 26, ©AP Photo; page 27, ©AP
Photo/Dave Martin; page 28, ©david ross/Alamy

Library of Congress Cataloging-in-Publication Data
Kelley, K. C.
Golf / by K.C. Kelley.
    p. cm.–(Innovation in sports)
Includes index.
ISBN-13: 978-1-60279-262-3
ISBN-10: 1-60279-262-3
1. Golf–Juvenile literature. 2. Golf–Equipment and supplies–Juvenile
literature. 3. Golfers–Juvenile literature. I. Title. II. Series.
GV968.K45 2009
796.352–dc22   2008002045

Cherry Lake Publishing would like to acknowledge the work of
The Partnership for 21st Century Skills.
Please visit www.21stcenturyskills.org for more information.

CONTENTS

Chapter One
History of Golf 4

Chapter Two
Developing the Rules 8

Chapter Three
Golf Balls 12

Chapter Four
Golf Club Technology 17

Chapter Five
Golf's Great Innovators 24

Glossary 30
For More Information 31
Index 32
About the Author 32

CHAPTER ONE

History of Golf

Today, people from all over the world enjoy playing golf and working on their skills.

There is nothing quite like hitting a long drive off the tee on a beautiful summer day. Golf is a popular game that combines great physical activity with the outdoors. Golf is also one of the oldest sports in the world. It is a game with many traditions, rules, and customs.

People disagree on the origins of golf. Some say that a golf-like game may have been played in China as early as the 11th century. Most people trace the game's beginnings back to Scotland in the 15th century. Legend has it that long ago, Scottish shepherds created the game to help pass the time. The shepherds whacked stones with their sticks, aiming the stones at trees and holes. This game caught on quickly, and people began playing various versions of the game throughout Europe.

As golf's popularity grew, people wanted to play on a field that was designed specifically for golf. By the 1600s, planned golf **courses** were being laid out in Scottish pastures alongside the sea. New courses were built on the many rolling grasslands of the British Isles. Soon golf courses were being built across Europe.

By the 1700s, golfers were arguing about the rules. Every course had its own way of playing the game. Organization was needed. In St. Andrews, Scotland, a group of high-ranking citizens banded together to found The Royal and Ancient Golf Club of St. Andrews (The R&A) in 1754. They wrote down a set of official rules for the sport for all to follow. Many of those early rules are still in use today.

The sport grew quickly once everyone agreed on how to play. Soon each golf club had its own champions. Golf clubs wanted to send their best players to compete against other golf clubs. Soon these players began to organize matches and tournaments to play other clubs. In 1860, the first British Open was played at the Prestwick Golf Club in Scotland. Clubs from all over

The Royal and Ancient Golf Club of St. Andrews has a special place in golf history. The first rules for the game were created there.

Great Britain sent their champions to play each other at the Open. Willie Park Sr. of Scotland was the first British Open winner.

By the turn of the century, some players were finding that they could make money playing the game. But where did they get the money? The answer: **sponsors**. A sponsor would put up the "purse," or prize money, to attract top golfers to his club. A tournament, usually lasting four days, would be held at the sponsor's club.

The golfer with the best score would win the most money. These tournaments attracted a lot of fans, spectators, and great golfers.

Golf arrived in the United States in the late 1800s. The first golf club was formed near New York City in 1888. The United States Golf Association (USGA) was formed in 1894. In 1916, the **Professional** Golf Association of America (PGA) was founded. In 1968, the PGA founded the PGA Tour, today's top circuit of golf tournaments. The best golfers in the world come to the United States to play in PGA tournaments that offer the best prize money.

But golf wasn't always popular in America. There was a time when only those who were wealthy could play the game. But golf hit a growing spurt in the late 1990s with the debut of Tiger Woods. As today's top golfer, Tiger is one of the world's most famous sportsmen. His popularity has sparked a new generation of young players.

21st Century Content

Today, the men's PGA Tour includes players from Australia, Ireland, England, Germany, Spain, and even Fiji. The Ladies Professional Golf Association hosts the women's LPGA tour, and the nation of Sweden has captured many top titles on this tour. In recent years, one country's players are making a huge impact. Since the early 2000s, South Korean players have swarmed onto the scene. Among the top players from this golf-crazy country are Se Ri Pak, Jeong Jang, Seon Hwa Lee, and Mi Hyun Kim. These players prove that golf continues to be a global sport.

CHAPTER TWO

Developing the Rules

Can I move a rock that's blocking my shot? How many clubs can I carry in my golf bag? What happens if my ball lands in a pond? Golf seems like a simple game: take your club, hit the ball, find it, and hit it again. But lots of things can happen during a round, and golfers need to know what the rules are.

The first documented rules were written down in 1744 in Leith, Scotland. Ten years later, The R&A became the top club. The R&A's rules soon were recognized as the "official" rules of golf. As new issues came up, The R&A would meet and make its ruling. All golfers and golf clubs were **obliged** to follow any new rules. By 1899, their rules were adopted by the U.S. Golf Association (USGA), finally uniting the golf world.

Hitting the ball out of a bunker can be a challenge.

In golf, the key rule to remember is to "play the ball as it lies." A player must always hit the ball where it lands—whether it is on sand (called a bunker), in high grass (called the **rough**), or on the mowed grass of the "fairway" (the most desirable place for playing the ball). New rules are written all the time to address new issues that come up. For instance, there were no electric golf carts until 1962. An engineer named Merlin Halvorson invented this small vehicle to make playing golf take less

Golfers are expected to be considerate of one another. For instance, it is polite to stand off the green while a fellow golfer prepares to putt.

time. The rules then had to address situations like "What happens if my shot hits a golf cart?" or "What happens to my ball if it lands in a muddy tire track?" The R&A and the USGA have established rules to address these situations.

Another key issue that the rules must constantly deal with is golf equipment. Innovative new equipment and technology are constantly being developed. With each new invention or type of gear, the rules have to be adjusted. The rules help to organize and regulate changes to gear, such as new golf balls or golf clubs. The goal in all of this rule making is to keep the game fair and honest for all players.

Golf also has a set of "unwritten" rules known as golf **etiquette**. Golfers are expected to behave themselves on the course. Players do not disturb other players during a swing, and they do not damage the golf course. For example, if they send a clump of grass flying when they swing their club, they are expected to return it to its original spot. Golf is an honorable game, and the rules make sure it stays that way.

Most golf courses today have 18 holes, made up of a front nine and a back nine. Why 18 holes? The first courses had everything from 5 to 12 to 22 holes! The R&A's course had 18 holes. And since The R&A was the model golf club, all future golf clubs were built with 18 holes.

Life & Career Skills

In most sports, referees, umpires, or other officials make sure the rules are followed. In golf, the golfers call penalties on themselves. This honor system has long been a part of the game. One Hall of Fame golfer was a model for honesty. In 1925, Bobby Jones was competing in the final playoff of the U.S. Open. While setting up to take his next shot from the rough, his club caused the ball to move slightly. No other players saw the incident. Jones immediately went over to the officials and called a penalty on himself. Although he ended up losing the U.S. Open by only one stroke, his high personal standards maintained the integrity of the game. Today, the USGA's sportsmanship award is called the Bob Jones Award.

CHAPTER THREE

The Golf Ball

The golf ball has gone through a series of innovations. Each innovation seeks to solve one problem: how can we make a ball that flies straight and long and is still long lasting?

The first balls were solid and made out of carved rock or wood. But these balls were not very **durable** or safe. By the 1400s, golf ball makers came up with a brilliant solution. They sewed small leather pouches and then stuffed them with wet feathers from ducks or geese. As the feathers dried, they expanded, making the ball tight and firm. Known as featheries, these balls were the standard for hundreds of years.

Featheries worked for a while, but golfers began to complain about the design. It was always hard to make a perfectly round featherie ball, so no shot was ever

Golf ball design has undergone many changes through the years.

accurate. When playing in wet conditions, the ball's laces would get wet. This would cause the ball to burst open at the seams upon impact. Also, featheries were expensive and hard to make. Golfers began tinkering with the ball, looking for one that would go farther and last longer than the featherie.

Today's golf balls are made from hard plastic and have dimpled patterns.

In 1848, Scottish golfer Robert Adams Paterson created a golf ball out of squishy stuff called gutta-percha, which came from a tree in India. Paterson molded the gutta-percha like clay and then hardened it with heat. He found that the "guttie" flew farther than the feathery. The guttie was an instant hit. Golfers also discovered something else. Unlike the featherie, the guttie flew straighter later in a round of golf. Why? They figured out that the nicks and cuts to the smooth surface actually helped the ball fly better. Soon dozens of patterns of cuts and slices were put on the gutties. Golfers and ball makers continued looking for the pattern that would create the smoothest flight.

The next golf ball innovation came from America. Dentist Coburn Haskell and Goodrich rubber engineer Bertram G. Work wanted to make rubber a part of the golf ball design. To do this, they wrapped a small rubber ball with yards and yards of rubber bands. They then covered this bouncy ball with the old, familiar guttie. This new design created better spin and feel on the ball. A victory by Alex Herd at the 1902 British Open using this new ball convinced everyone to dump the old-fashioned gutties and adopt the rubber-band ball.

One man managed to find a ball design that helped create the smoothest flight. In 1905, ball maker William Taylor applied for a patent on his new dimpled golf ball.

21st Century Content

Golfers don't try to hit golf balls into the water, but sometimes it happens! What becomes of all those underwater golf balls? Smart businessmen have turned them into money. Using scuba gear and other tools, they gather up the balls, dry them, and then sell them to golfers looking for practice balls. Water-soaked balls aren't good enough for regular play, but they work fine on the practice range. Cargo carriers full of recovered balls are often sold to courses in Japan and China for thousands of dollars!

This was quickly shown to be the best solution yet. These dimples, or tiny indentations, made the air flow smoothly around the ball as it flew. Today, all golf balls have some sort of pattern of dimples.

In the 1960s, when plastic came on the scene, new plastic balls were made. The most successful of these were made of two pieces: a solid core and a thin outer shell. The two-piece plastic ball remains the standard.

Today, the golf ball industry is massive, with nearly a billion dollars spent each year on balls and related products alone. Scientists and companies continue their search for products that can give golfers more distance and accuracy. One thing is certain—golf balls have come a long way since rocks and featheries!

CHAPTER FOUR

Golf Club Technology

Much thought has gone into the development of golf balls. But what about the clubs we use to hit the ball? Believe it or not, golf clubs have seen many innovations throughout the history of the game. The pursuit of the perfect golf club has dominated some of golf's greatest minds.

Golf clubs of the past usually featured wooden heads. Players found these clubs to be easily breakable.

The first clubs were made from wood. Craftsmen who were skilled at making bows and arrows carved pieces of wood into different shapes to make clubs. Players realized that they couldn't use one club for every type of shot. Different shots needed different clubs. A club with a flat face would hit the ball long and low. A club with a tilted face would hit the ball high in an arc.

Players began complaining about the wooden clubs' heads. Many times, these heads would break, making golf a very expensive game. Blacksmiths soon got into the act, making iron heads that could be attached to the wooden sticks, now called **shafts**. Iron heads were more durable and didn't break like the wooden heads. Another key innovation came about in the early 1900s, when grooves were cut into the clubfaces. As the ball hit these grooves, it spun. This backspin on the ball can help guide a shot in a particular direction.

By the first British Open, golf clubs had been given unusual names. Players in the early 1900s started a hole with a brassie. Then, out on the fairway, they might use a mashie or a spade. A niblick was used for the final shot to the green. Eventually, the names of the clubs were standardized with numbers. For example, a cleek was a 1- or 2-iron, while a mashie was a 5-iron. Clubs are still numbered today.

Today, golf clubs are made with metal or graphite shafts. These shafts give greater flex and allow golfers to swing more easily through the ball.

Players continued to look for clubs that were more durable. In 1925, metal shafts replaced the hickory wood that was popular. Metal shafts didn't break nearly as easily as wooden ones, and they were easier to **mass-produce**. With this particular innovation, the rule makers got involved, making sure that all new clubs followed rules they laid down.

For the next few decades, the "irons" changed as new materials and designs were used. The "woods," or drivers, however, didn't change as much. Until the 1990s, all drivers still had wooden club heads, with metal shafts. But the introduction of **titanium** and **graphite** woods changed golf equipment overnight. Woods made of metal, such as Callaway's Big Bertha model, gave the best players a way to add enormous length to their drives. The metal facing gave the ball a spring, while the large, yet lightweight head put more power behind the ball. Even everyday players were suddenly "long off the tee."

Golf's rule makers, along with the USGA, tried to ban the clubs. They felt that players were getting too much of an advantage on the course. They soon found that these new, flashy clubs were too popular. They did, however, put limits on the size and "springiness" of the clubs. The quest continues today for bigger and more powerful drivers that are still within the rules. These

Callaway's Big Bertha golf club revolutionized golf. It allows even average players to hit the ball farther than ever.

clubs are still called woods, even though they are made of metal now.

The putter is the last club a player uses to make those final, crucial short strokes to "hole out." Putters have been through a lot of innovation. A visit to a golf store will show you that there are many different designs for

Modern putters help players make precise shots on the green.

putters. But putters weren't always this varied. The first putters were simple iron blades on wooden shafts. Today, space-age metals, endless testing by scientists, and new designs from pros and **amateurs** alike all come into play in putting. No one has invented the perfect putter, but that doesn't mean they aren't all still trying.

Life & Career Skills

Golfers are always trying to improve their swings. They work with coaches, read books, and practice for hours. One recent innovation is video and computer swing training. Golfers are videotaped from many angles, and a computer then analyzes their swing. By seeing themselves swing on video and analyzing the swing using computer programs, golfers can learn what areas they need to improve or change. Who knows how good 1920s amateur legend Bobby Jones might have been with a video camera to help him!

Golf's Great Innovators

Players of all ages take part in the game of golf.

Many people have had a big impact on the development and growth of golf over the years. Some made their marks on the courses, while others changed the game with their creative designs. Let's meet a few of the game's innovators.

Old Tom Morris

Golf's first legendary figure was a player, a course designer, and a leader in spreading the word about the game. After growing up and working in

This statue of Old Tom Morris is featured on a golf course in Las Vegas, Nevada. Morris not only played golf well, but he helped improve golf course design.

St. Andrews, Tom Morris Sr. worked as a greenkeeper at Prestwick, where he helped set up the first British Open in 1860. He played in every British Open from 1860 until 1896, winning it four times. He became the greenkeeper at the legendary R&A in 1865, and his ideas about course design and maintenance influenced hundreds of future designers.

Bobby Jones

The first real American golf superstar, Bobby Jones remained an amateur his entire career. He was the first player to win the British and U.S. Opens as well as the U.S. and British Amateur championships. This feat, in 1930, remains known as "the grand slam." After earning his law degree, he retired from golf when he was only 28 years old. He later helped found the August National Golf Club in Georgia. This famous club is home to the Masters, golf's most challenging annual tournament.

Bobby Jones, shown here holding his U.S. Open trophy, won all four major golf tournaments in 1930.

Ely Callaway's company continues to develop top-of-the-line equipment for golfers everywhere.

Ely Callaway

Few individuals have had as much impact on golf club design as Georgia-born Ely Callaway. Already a successful businessman in his 60s, he bought a small golf club company in 1982. Under his leadership, Callaway Golf revolutionized the game. The oversized Big Bertha driver helped kick off a decade-long golf boom in the 1990s, giving everyday players the chance to hit as far as some pros. The company's Odyssey putter remains one of the most popular, and even Callaway golf balls are now making an impact on the game.

Tiger Woods is considered one of the greatest golfers ever. His popularity has encouraged a whole new generation to start playing the game.

Tiger Woods

Combine an intense work ethic, natural talent, great golf gear, and an interesting background, and you've got Tiger Woods, the most famous name in golf. Tiger began winning golf tournaments against older opponents by the time he was in grade school. In his early teens, he won three U.S. Junior titles and then three U.S. Amateur titles. After turning pro in 1996, he stunned the sports world in 1997 when, at the age of 21, he won the Masters by an astonishing 12 strokes. He's just gotten better since, winning 13 of golf's "**majors**" and nine PGA Player of the Year awards. His mixed Asian–African American background and great personality off the course have attracted a younger generation of golfers and golf fans.

Learning & Innovation Skills

Golf is an individual sport. Every two years, however, the top golfers in the United States and Europe face off as teams. In the Ryder Cup competition, which began in 1927, golfers from each team gather at one course and play a series of group events. They pair up with teammates to try to beat the other side. Golfers who usually play against each other are suddenly rooting for each other. These events get a lot of attention from fans and can end in very dramatic fashion. The United States dominated the competition for many years, but in the 2000s, Europe's team has won several Ryder Cups.

Why do you think golfers like to compete in the Ryder Cup? What are the advantages and disadvantages of playing golf as part of a team?

Glossary

amateurs (AM-uh-churz) people who do something without getting paid for doing it

courses (KORSS-iz) the places where golf is played

durable (DUR-uh-buhl) something that is strong and will last a long time

etiquette (ET-uh-ket) a way of behaving properly

graphite (GRAF-ite) a composite material that has carbon fibers for reinforcement

majors (MAY-jurz) in pro golf, the four top tournaments: U.S. Open, British Open, PGA Championship, and the Masters

mass-produce (MASS pruh-DOOSS) to make many of an identical product at the same time

obliged (uh-BLIJED) forced to

practice range (PRAK-tiss RAYNJ) an area near a golf course where golfers can hit many balls at targets without having to walk a course (or retrieve the balls!)

professional (pruh-FESH-uh-nuhl) a person who performs a job or plays a sport for money

rough (RUHF) the area on the edges of a golf fairway where the grass is longer and harder to hit a ball out of

shafts (SHAFTS) the sticklike part of a golf club, from the handle to the face

sponsors (SPON-surz) companies that pay a team or a player money to endorse their product

titanium (tie-TAY-nee-uhm) a strong, lightweight metal

For More Information

BOOKS

Golf: Eyewitness Companions. New York: DK Publishing, 2005.

Smith, Ryan A. *Made in the USA—Golf Balls*. Farmington Hills, MI: Blackbirch Press, 2005.

Woods, Bob. *Tiger Woods*. Mankato, MN: The Child's World, 2008.

WEB SITES

Junior Links.com Games
www.juniorlinks.com/games/triviagame.cfm
Play a fun golf trivia game for kids

PGA of America
www.pga.com
Get the latest news, info, and footage of your favorite professional golfers

Index

August National Golf Club, 26

Big Bertha drivers, 20, 27–28
Bob Jones Award, 11
brassies, 18
British Open, 5–6, 15, 18, 25, 26
bunkers, 9

Callaway, Ely, 27–28
Callaway Golf company, 20, 27–28
cleeks, 18
computers, 23

dimples, 15–16
drivers, 20–21, 27–28

equipment, 10–11
etiquette, 11

fairway, 9, 18
featheries, 12–14

golf balls, 11, 12–16, 28
golf carts, 9–10

golf clubs, 11, 17–18, 20–21, 23
golf courses, 5, 11, 25
graphite, 20
gutties, 15

Halvorson, Merlin, 9–10
Haskell, Coburn, 15
Herd, Alex, 15
holes, 11
honor system, 11

irons, 20

Jang, Jeong, 7
Jones, Bobby, 11, 26

Kim, Mi Hyun, 7

Ladies Professional Golf Association (LPGA), 7
Lee, Seon Hwa, 7
LPGA Tour, 7

"majors" tournaments, 29
mashies, 18
Masters tournament, 26, 29

Morris, Tom, Sr., 24–25

niblicks, 18

Odyssey putters, 28
origins, 4–5

Pak, Se Ri, 7
Park, Willie, Sr., 6
Paterson, Robert Adams, 15
penalties, 11
PGA Tour, 7
Prestwick Golf Club, 5
prize money. See purse.
Professional Golf Association of America (PGA), 7, 29
"purse," 6, 7
putters, 21, 23

rough, 9
Royal and Ancient Golf Club of St. Andrews (R&A), 5, 8, 10, 11, 25
rules, 5, 8–9, 10–11, 20
Ryder Cup tournament, 29

shafts, 18, 20, 23
shepherds, 5
shots, 10, 12–13, 18
spades, 18
sponsors, 6
swings, 11, 23

Taylor, William, 15–16
titanium, 20
tournaments, 5–7, 11, 15, 18, 25, 26, 29
training, 23

United States Golf Association (USGA), 7, 8, 10, 20
U.S. Open, 11, 26

video, 23

water hazards, 16
woods. See drivers.
Woods, Tiger, 7, 29
Work, Bertram G., 15

About the Author

K. C. Kelley has written many books and magazine articles about sports for young readers. He has played golf for many years (though not as well as the people in this book!) and now enjoys playing with his son, Conor. They live in Santa Barbara, California.

Golf